A Brief History of Bath County, Virginia

Jean Graham McAllister

BIBLIOLIFE

A Brief History

OF

Bath County
Virginia

——————

PREPARED

by

JEAN GRAHAM McALLISTER

Under the auspices of the County
School Board and the Board of
Supervisors of the County.

——————

PRICE 10 CENTS

Brief History

OF

Bath County Virginia

*When Was the Virginia Assembly First Petitioned,
Regarding Surveys in Bath County?*

In 1727 a petition was sent to the Governor and
Council requesting that "fifty thousand acres of land
in one or more tracts on the head branches of the
James River to the West and Northwestward of the
Cowpasture," might be taken up and settled upon.
The signers were: Beverly Robinson, Robert Brooks,
William Lynn and Robert and William Lewis. The
petition does not seem to have been acted upon.
However, it is interesting to note that as early as
1727 the Cowpasture River had already acquired its
present name.

2. *When Were the First Surveys Made in Bath
County?*

It seems probable that no settlers appeared in
Bath County before 1743. The first surveys were
made on September 26, 1745 for Adam Dickinson
by Thomas and Andrew Lewis.

3. *What Was the Menace to Peaceful Living in the Days of the Early Settlers*

The Indians, the Aboriginees of America, watched with great jealously the coming of the white men from across the sea. And it must be admitted that the Red Man was many times treated unfairly by the British. Until 1748 the Alleghany Front formed the Western frontier of Virginia. The Indians visited the early settlers in Bath and were always treated with suspicion by them. The Scotch-Irish despised the Indian and saw no reason why their race should have·any rights. In turn the Indians inflicted cruel warfare upon the whites—making the daily life of the early settlers almost a thing of dread. And not until the decisive victory over Pontiac in 1763, when the Indians were defeated, was this menace to civilization removed.

4. *What Were the Names of the Indian Forts in Bath and Where Were They Situated?*

Fort Dickinson on the Cowpasture seems to have been the main strong hold. The exact site is not marked, but it stood in the river bottom a half mile north of Nimrod Hall. Fort Dinwiddie, another famous Indian Fort, was located on the Jackson River one mile north of Fassifern Farm. It is interesting to note that this fort was visited by General Washington in his Southern tour of inspection in 1755. Fort George stood on the·Bullpasture near the Clover Creek

Mill. Fort Mann stood at the bottom of Falling Springs Run. The field in which Fort George was located has never been plowed, and one can easily trace the lines of a stockade and covered way. Several houses were also capable of fortification to repel the Indian. But despite the many forts the settlers were often careless and suffered severe losses as a result. Many of the inhabitants were killed, others were captured—some returning after long absences with the Indians.

5. Where Were the First Settlements in Bath?

In 1745 in the Valley of the Cowpasture, toward the North, we find the first settlements. These surveys include the very desirable river bottom lands. In 1746 the surveyors engaged in parcelling out the fertile tracts of Jackson River. The largest tract was for William Jackson. It was for him that the Jackson River was named. Adam Dickenson owned land on the Jackson River, also James Ewing, William Jameson and Archibald Elliott. The Lewis surveys included lands immediately below Bullpasture Gap— two tracts on Jackson River and four on Back Creek.

6. Why Do the Historians Speak of "Greater Bath"

From 1790-1822 the County embraced a great deal more territory than its present area. Thus we find that the historian speak of the "Bath Area" when he speaks of the present boundaries of the County, and of

"Greater Bath" when he intends to indicate the period between 1790-1822.

7. From What Counties Was Bath Formed?

An act of the Assembly passed December 14, 1790 created Bath County, from the Counties of Augusta, Botetourt and Greenbrier.

8. What Counties Bound Bath County?

Bath is bounded on the North by Highland, on the East by Augusta and Rockbridge, on the South by Alleghany and on the West by Pocahontas and Greenbrier Counties.

9. Describe the County from a Geographical Point of View?

Bath is essentially a mountainous County, with long narrow valleys. The Western boundry is the central ridge of the Appalachians. It divides the waters; those running to the Atlantic and those coursing towards the Mississippi. Until West Virginia separated from Virginia Bath County lay near the center of the State. It is now on the Western border. The County is divided into two main valleys; those of the Cowpasture and Jackson's River. The important sub-valleys are in the West: Warm Springs Valley, Big and Little Back Creek Valleys. In the East: Dry Run, Stuart's Creek, Porter's Mill Creek and Padd's Creek. The mountains of Bath are very symetrical, and the scenery unusually beautiful. The climate, as a whole, is very delightful. The altitude of 2200 feet insures against intensive heat in summer, and the mountain ridges on both sides protect the valley inhabitants from the more violent storms visited upon the coast dwellers and those people living west of the Alleghanies. The Warm Springs Mountain forms the natural division of the County.

10. *What is the Area of Bath County?*

548 square miles or 352,720 acres.

The outline of the County follows that of a quadrangle, the four corners pointing very nearly North, East, South and West.

11. *When Was the County Formed?*

December 14, 1790 the Virginia Assembly passed an act which created Bath County (act found in Morton's History.) The first court in Bath County convened on May 10, 1791 at the home of Margaret Lewis, widow of Captain John Lewis, at Warm Springs. The justices present on the opening day were the following:—John Bollar, J. Dean, J. Poage, William Poage, Samuel Vance and John Wilson. The first sheriff was Sampson Matthews and Charles Cameron, the first clerk. Their bond was set at 1,000 lbs. ($3,333.33). William Poage was the first surveyor and Samuel Vance the first coroner. The Attorneys were John Cotton, James Reed, and Archibald Stuart. The members of the first Grand Jury were: Joseph Mayse, foreman, Samuel Black, Thomas Brode. John

Dilley, James Hamilton, James Hughart, Owen Kelley, John Lynch, John McClung, Samuel McDonnald, John Montgomery, Joseph Rhea, William Rider, Robert Stuart and Stephen Wilson.

12. *What Are the Chief Crops?*

Hay, Wheat, Corn and Oats are the chief products. The fruits grown most extensively in Bath are apples, pears, plums and peaches. The smaller berries, also abound; namely, blackberries, huckle-berries, etc

13. *Is Bath Fitted to Agricultural Pursuits?*

Bath is particularly adapted to sheep and cattle raising. Its facilities for grazing are excellent, grass growing in any cleared piece of ground. The soil in the valleys is rich and with its splendid water supply becomes easily a most fertile garden spot. A large percent of the citizens are engaged in farming.

14. *What Minerals are Found in Bath*

Manganese is found in the mountains, and fossil ore with a thickness of two feet has been found in the mountain east of Warm Springs. Bath County lies in the iron ore district of the Western Blue Ridge, but little has been done to develop this ore so far.

15. *What Are the Chief Industries in Bath?*

Grazing, farming, and forest product enterprises. The saw mills are numerous, and a broom factory has recently been established. Important lumbermen have recently bought large tracts in Bath.

16. *What Are the Qualities of the Water?*

The Springs in Bath County are famous throughout the United States for their remarkable curative qualities. At Hot Springs we find a spring of 106 degrees. One spring is magnesia, another soda, a third sulphur, etc., "six flowing fountains." (M) The principal minerals in these waters are calcium, magnesium, sodium and potassium. The waters are beneficial particularly in rheumatic conditions. The "bubbling pools" at Warm Springs have a temperature of 98 degrees. The Healing Springs waters are bottled and sent to various parts of the Country. Bolar Springs in "Great Valley" is noted for its effectiveness in skin diseases, temperature 74 degrees. We find alum water at Bath Alum and Wallawhatoolah, with Sulphur Springs at Millboro Springs. It is taken for granted that the thermal qualities of the healing waters of Bath were known to the Indians and many legends are told concerning them.

17. *What Large Corporation Has Done Much to Add to the Attraction of Bath?*

The Virginia Hot Springs Company, a large corporation of which Mr. M. E. Ingalls is President, bought the property on which the Homestead at Hot Spring is situated, in 1890. The same Company later bought the Warm and Healing Springs property.

They have connected the three places by a splendid macadam road.

The Bath house at Hot Springs is a modernly equipped with the most approved methods for administering medicinal baths. The "cures" abroad have been studied, and the patient is advised by doctors of nation-wide reputation. The bath attendants .are Swedish. The company has also added to the natural beauty of the place, making it a pleasure resort as well as a sanatarium. The hotel is one of the best appointed in the Country. The golf links and the tennis courts are excellent. The drives and trails lead to fascinating spots. The Warm Springs is still the old fashioned resort of 50 years ago. The Healing Springs is a pretty, modernly equipped, resort. The Virginia Hot Springs Company has brought great wealth into the county and given employment to hundreds of people. Their dairy is noted for the freshness of its products and the Homestead poultry farm is one of the very best equipped of its kind.

18. From What Race Are the Inhabitants of Bath Descended?

Scotch-Irish Men of Ulster, Ireland, who left that Country to escape the tyranny of the crown. These people were of a hardy race, earnest, industrious, seeking freedom of religious thought.

19. What Was the Professed Religion of the Early Settlers?

The early settlers adhered to the doctrines of the Presbyterian Church.

20. *What Is The Legend of Selim?*

Between 1764 and 1774 Samuel Given was hunting in the woods near Warm Springs one day and saw what he mistook for an animal. Instead it turned out to be a man in the last stages of starvation. Given was kind to the man and took him home where with good food and rest he soon recovered his faculties. He called himself Selim. He was made welcome at the home of Captain John Dickenson near Windy Cove and spent some months there. His family were Algerines and were people of wealth in the Barbary States. They had sent their son to Constantinople for higher education While he was returning home his ship was captured by a Spanish man-of-war. He was then put on a ship bound for New Orleans. From' New Orleans Selim was taken to the Shawnee settlement on Scioto. He escaped from the Indians and was making his way east to the English settlements when found by Given. On being taken to Staunton by Dickenson the Algerine was much attracted by John Craig, the Presbyterian minister and asked leave to go home with him There he became informed of the doctrines of Christianity. He was baptised at the Old Stone Church in Augusta. Finally the longing to return to his own people made him decide to leave his many friends He was aided by Mr. Craig and others and was given a letter to Robert Carter, mem-

ber of the House of Burgesses. Years later he returned, his mind in disorder. It seemed that his father had
been much angered at his giving up the faith of Mo-
hammed. He went to Warm Springs and was de-
lighted with a Greek Testament given him by a minister named Templeton. He died in 1805.

20A. *Who Was John Craig?*

John Craig was the first minister to preach in
Bath County. He preached on the Cowpasture River
as early as 1749.

21. *What of Alexander Craighead*

Craighead followed Craig, buying land in Bath
County. He did not remain here long. Many of his
congregation badly frightened by the frequent Indian raids decided to move to North Carolina, whence
Craighead had already gone. He thought by moving
there that his people would at least have religious
liberty. The Church of England still being the established order in Virginia.

22. *What Do You Know of the Two Moravian
Priests?*

A journal kept by the two Moravian Priests gives
us quite a picture of the conditions in which the early
settlers lived. These good men travelled from Penn-
sylvania to the Dunkard settlement on New River
administering to the spiritual needs of the settlers of
German birth. They journeyed into this Valley in

1749 and crossed Warm Springs Mountain, spending the night, as nearly as we can ascertain, near where the toll gate now stands. The settlers seem to have been chary of taking in strangers, but on the whole the two priests met with kindness. They found the whites living under the crudest conditions, wearing animal skins for clothing, eating coarse food, such as bear meat, and spending most of the day hunting. Dr. Thomas Walker, in a diary of July 1750, says that the settlers on Jackson's River "are very hospitable and would be better able to support themselves were it not for the great number of the Indian warriors, who take what they want from them, much to their prejudice."

23. *When Was the First Church Built and Where?*

The Windy Cove Presbyterian Church on the Cowpasture River, the first building of which was erected as early as 1752, was the first Protestant church built West of the Shenandoah Mountain.

24. *Why Should Bath People Feel An Especial Interest in the Battle of Point Pleasant? Give Date of Battle with Main Points.*

The Battle of Point Pleasant has come to be looked upon as the beginning of the Revolutionary War. This engagement took place in 1774 at Point Pleasant on the Kanawha Rivers. The Virginians under Andrew and Charles Lewis advanced to meet the oncoming hordes of Red Men. The Indian Chief was Cornstalk of the Shawnee. Dunmore failed to put in an appearance at the appointed meeting place. The discipline in the Virginia Army became slack and nearly resulted in a complete surprise of the Virginians by the Red men. But fortunately they were warned just in time. The men fell to work erecting a breast-work of trees. The battle commenced, the bitter struggle continuing till dusk amid the fierce cries of the opposing forces. General Lewis proved himself a real strategist, his maneuver turning the tide of battle in favor of the whites. Unable to offer open warfare Lewis sent three companies up the Kanawha, then up a little tributary, thus enabling them to attack the flank of the Indians from the rear. This maneuver led the Chief to believe that the Whites were being reinforced, and so he decided upon a retreat, but all the time issuing such threats of violence that Lewis felt that they must have reinforcements. Such was not the case, however, and so the battle of Point Pleasant ended in a decisive victory for the whites. Their victory cost them dear, while the loss of the Indians was almost negligible. Col. Charles Lewis, whose home was in Bath Area, a gallant soldier and a gentleman, was mortally wounded during the battle. Among the Captains under General Lewis were: John Skidmore, Samuel Wilson, Andrew Lockridge and John Lewis, John Dickehson and George Matthews all land owners in the present County of Bath. The final treaty between the Indians and Whites was not effected until the following year after the Battle of Point Pleasant. And it was made between the Americans and Indians, the former harboring still a distrust of the Tory Governor who had failed them in a critical time of their need.

25. *What of Bath During the Revolution?*

There were no battles fought in Bath during the Revolutionary War, but her men followed the armies elsewhere. The first company, of which we have already spoken was raised in 1774 by Capt. John Lewis, and placed under Col. Charles Lewis. 1780 saw the enrollment of a company at Warm Springs which served throughout the war, with Capt. Wm. Long in command. This company was in the line of battle at the time of Cornwallis' surrender.

The old registers at the Warm Springs Hotel contain the names of many distinguished Revolutionary officers. Among the names of the Bath men who are known to have held rank in the Revolutionary army are the following: Robert McCreery, John Bollar, David Gwinn, Sampson Matthews, Thomas Hicklin, Wm. Kincaid, John Brown, Charles Cameron, Robert Thompson, Wm. McCreery, Wm. Wright, Joseph - Gwin, John Oliver, Samuel Black, James Bratton, Samuel McClintic, Robert McFarland, Thomas Cardwell, Jonathan Humphrey, and Moses McClintic.

26. *What Year Did the Virginia Legislature Adjourn to Meet at Warm Springs and Why?*

During the Revolutionary war the British advanced into Albemarle County. The approach of Tarleton and his men so disturbed the peace of the Virginia Legislature then sitting in Charlottesville that they moved to Staunton on June 7, 1781. They met the next Sunday and hearing that the British were still in pursuit adjourned to meet at Warm Springs. The alarm was false and the members who fled toward Lexington and Warm Springs, (Patrick Henry among the latter) returned to Staunton.

27. *Did Bath Men Fight in the War of* 1812?

Yes, but no one has yet compiled the facts.

28. *Did Bath Men Fight in the Civil War? Name Regiment, etc.*

The Bath Squadron, composed of two companies, belonged to the Eleventh Cavalry. Capt. A. G. Mc-Chesney was in command of Company F. and Capt. F. A. Dangerfield in command of Company G. The men in these Companies saw service during the whole period of the long war.

Bath did not lie in the fighting area but there were skirmishes in the Millboro and Williamsville Districts. Also a remnant of the Federal Army passed through the county, giving the Bath citizens a taste of the horrors of invasion.

In May, 1861, the first company, before it marched away, was presented with a beautiful Confederate flag made by the devoted women of Bath. This flag was received on behalf of the company by Capt. A. T. Richards with these words "We will cherish it as we will our wives and sweethearts!"

Even in Bath all the men were not Confederates. A striking incident is demonstrated in the Terrill family. One brother, William R. Terrill, a graduate of West Point, served as Brigadier-General on the Union side, while another brother, Brigadier-General James B. Terrill, fought with the forces of his own State. L. P. Dangerfield, and a man in another command, were the first men to be wounded on the "Rebel" side. This occured in the engagement at Phillippi, West Virginia, where the Confederates were commanded by Col. Porterfield.

The 52nd infantry, in the brigade of General Edward Johnson and later serving under Stonewall Jackson, numbered many Bath Soldiers among its ranks. In Morton's History, page 152, will be found a roster with the names of most of the Bath soldiers who served during the Civil War. The hotels in the Warm Springs Valley were used as Confederate Hospitals.

29. *What Service Did Bath Render During the Great War?*

In every phase of the War work the county distinguished itself greatly. In every one of the drives, whether for the sale of War Saving stamps or the sale of bonds, it stood well at the head of the Virginia counties. Her contributions to the various charities evidenced a quick generous response which should fill the people with pride. For the success of these efforts the women·of Bath are largely entitled to the credit.

Her soldier boys served with faithfulness and distinction. *An avenue of trees, five miles in length, planted in memory of these boys, was dedicated and the memorial stone unveiled in July 1920, at which time the Attorney-General of Virginia and Senator Chauncey Depew delivered the addresses. It would require too much space to tell the story in detail, but a history of the work is being prepared for the Court records of the County.

30. Where is the County Seat?

Warm Springs is the County Seat of Bath and here Court convenes four times a year. Judge George K. Anderson is the judge.

Bath lies in the 10th congressional district. The county officers are as follows: Commonwealth's Attorney, County Clerk, Treasurer, Commissioner of the Revenues, Justices of the Peace for each District, Sheriff for the County with Deputies, Board of Supervisors and the Public School Board of Directors with the Superintendent of the County schools.

31. Why Has Fassifern A Special Significance?

On Fassifern Farm, situated five miles West of Warm Springs, stands the first Clerk's office used by Charles Cameron in 1791.

*These trees were donated and planted by the Virginia Hot Springs Company.

32. *What of the Early Schools?*

The early settlers were Scotch and ever since the Reformation in England these people have showed a decided interest in general education. The first mention of a school house in the Bath Area is in 1779. It was situated in Indian Draft near the basin of Stuart's Creek. The Pioneers of Bath were almost all able to read and write. Interest in the Public Schools of Virginia was slow to develop; the prevailing sentiment holding that education should be a private and not a public responsibility. However, in 1842 we find a petition by Patrick Malloy and fifty-seven other persons setting forth the inadequacy of the system. In 1846 a plan for free tuition was adopted and since then Virginia has continued to make rapid strides in the improvement of her schools. Bath County now has three well equipped high schools and the necessary number of graded schools.

33. *What Are Natural Points of Interest in Bath?*

West of Millboro Springs on the main road from that place to Warm Springs we find Blowing Cave, mentioned by Jefferson as a "natural curiosity." In the summer it expels cold air and in the winter draws in cold air. At Flag Rock, which is two and a half miles from Warm Springs, we have one of the most splendid views in the country. With an elevation of 3,500 feet it commands a wide expanse of territory. The Flowing Spring, located on Mr. Robert McClintic's farm near Williamsville, continues to baffle people as to its source. It flows for a while and then, with no warning whatever, ceases. The Cascades, one mile below Healing Springs is one of the most beautiful sights in the country. Flowing through a deep gorge about a mile in length and densely wooded, a little mountain stream forms one cascade after another, and so beautiful are the falls that the spectator is often speechless with delight. The Falls located just below the Alleghany line on the main road is another marvel of natural beauty. This cataract in Falling Springs Run leaps a depth of seventy feet.

34. *How Early Did the Springs Become Celebrated?*

In 1800 six thousand persons are said to have visited the neighboring springs in this section of Virginia. The Indians, of course, had found out the curative value of the waters long before this. Warm Springs, before the Civil War was the fashionable resort, the Hot Springs then being known as "Little Warm Springs." In 1822 we find in Memoirs of John Howe Peyton mention made of the delightful company assembled at the Warm Springs Hotel, Among the assemblage we find names of men prominent throughout the State. When we remember that the C. & O. branch now running into Hot Springs was not built until 1892, we realize what a journey it was to cross the mountains from the valley of Virginia. The stage coach was then in use.

Thomas Bullitt seems to have first appreciated the value of the Hot Springs and he and Andrew Lewis obtained a patent for the Hot Springs tract of 300 acres.

The first hotel was built on the site of the present hotel in 1766, parts of it standing until the fire on July 3, 1901. 1750 is given as the date when Dr. Thomas Walker visited Hot Springs and found six invalids there.

The Virginia Legislature granted a charter in 1793 permitting the owners to dispose of lots by lottery to form the town of Hot Baths. This scheme fell through. Dr. Thomas Goode in 1832 became possessor of the Virginia Hot Springs and it was under his management that the place acquired its enviable reputation.

35. Through What Channel is the County Endeavoring to Better the Health of Its Citizens?

At Hot Springs we find the Community House founded through the efforts of Miss Gladys Ingalls. The ladies around Hot Springs raise funds and make garments for use in the community. An operating room has been fitted out in memory of Dr. Henry S. Pole. The Community House now has a resident nurse, as well as a district nurse, who visits the people in their home.

Since the Great War the need of a district visiting

nurse has been realized throughout the county and through the Bath County Chapter of the American Red Cross this need has been supplied. Miss Hamilton, our first county nurse, is now engaged in giving the school children an examination thus, making them more fit for study and consequently better equipped for life. Nothing is more undermining to the general health than an ignorant carelessness in regard to infections of the eyes, nose, ear and throat.

It is hoped that the children will appreciate the efforts of the county in their behalf and that they will follow, most carefully, the instructions of the nurse.

36. *What of the Roads in Bath?*

In 1746 the Augusta County Court ordered that "a road be laid off and marked from the great lick in Cowpasture adjoining Col. Lewis' land to Andrew Hamilton in the Calf Pasture, and that Andrew Lewis and George Lewis mark out and lay off the same and make report to the next Court." The Indians had blazed trails long before this, and the herds of buffalo had also made passage-ways through the mountains. The first authorized road to Warm Springs was in 1763. Money was hard to procure for road building. Even in these days of presumed enlightenment it is often difficult to secure funds for the improvement of county roads.

The first roads were rough trails for horse-back riders, a striking contrast to the macadam boulevard that now connects Warm Springs and Healing Springs.

Good roads bring people together, improve trade and thus tend to the general happiness. The good roads movement throughout the State should be aided and abeted by every one.

37. What is the Present Population?

About 7,500.

This publication is, of necessity, but a sketch designed to touch lightly on some of the points of Bath history. It is hoped that it may awaken an interest which will result in rescuing from oblivion some of the fast disappearing stories of this section. It has been truthfully said that no part of America will more richly repay the student of history than the watershed of the Jackson and Cowpasture Rivers.

There are several recent publications on this subject, but none of them has done more than gather a few of the facts. Here is a delightful task for some of those who are today in our schools. Who will answer to the call?

LaVergne, TN USA
03 December 2009
165868LV00001B